Rupture

# Rupture

Poems by

Patricia Gray

*For John, wise counselor & friend.*
*Patricia Chapters*
*11/20/04*

Red Hen Press  Los Angeles

# Rupture

Copyright © 2005 by Patricia Gray

All Rights Reserved

No part of this book may be used or reproduced in any manner whatever without the prior written permission of both the publisher and author.

Typeset by Michael Vukadinovich

ISBN 1-888996-94-3
Library of Congress Catalog Card Number 2004095862

The City of Los Angeles Cultural Affairs Department, California Arts Council and the Los Angeles County Arts Commission partially support Red Hen Press.

Printed in Canada

First Edition

**Red Hen Press**
www.redhen.org

# Acknowledgments

These poems, or versions thereof, first appeared in the following publications: "Bicycling" in *Shenandoah*; "The Girl/The Girlie Magazine" in *Calyx* and *Anthology of Magazine Verse and Yearbook of American Poetry*; Sex and Breakfast" in *ELF*; "Blessing" in *Sunrust*; "Olivia: The Spiral between Men and Women" in *So to Speak* and *PoetryMagazine.com*; "Flesh and Sanity," "Mt. Bethany Cedar," and "Reading Your Letter on the Metro" in *Minimus*; "Flu, Spring Rain, and You" in *Cosmopolitan*; "To make a bow" in *Winners: A Retrospective of the Washington Prize*; "Calf Born in Snow" in *Cider Press Review*; "Mapping the Human Genome" in *Switched-On Gutenberg*; "Monument Water" and "Thin Air" in *WordWrights*; "Late in the Day" in *ForPoetry.com*; "Male Taken from Female" and "Contagious Magic" in *PoetryMagazine.com*.

My deepest, heartfelt thanks to colleagues and friends for their comments and support, and to Bread Loaf Writers Conference, and to the D.C. Commission on the Arts and Humanities for fellowships through the National Endowment for the Arts that allowed me to develop this book.

For Denny and Charlie

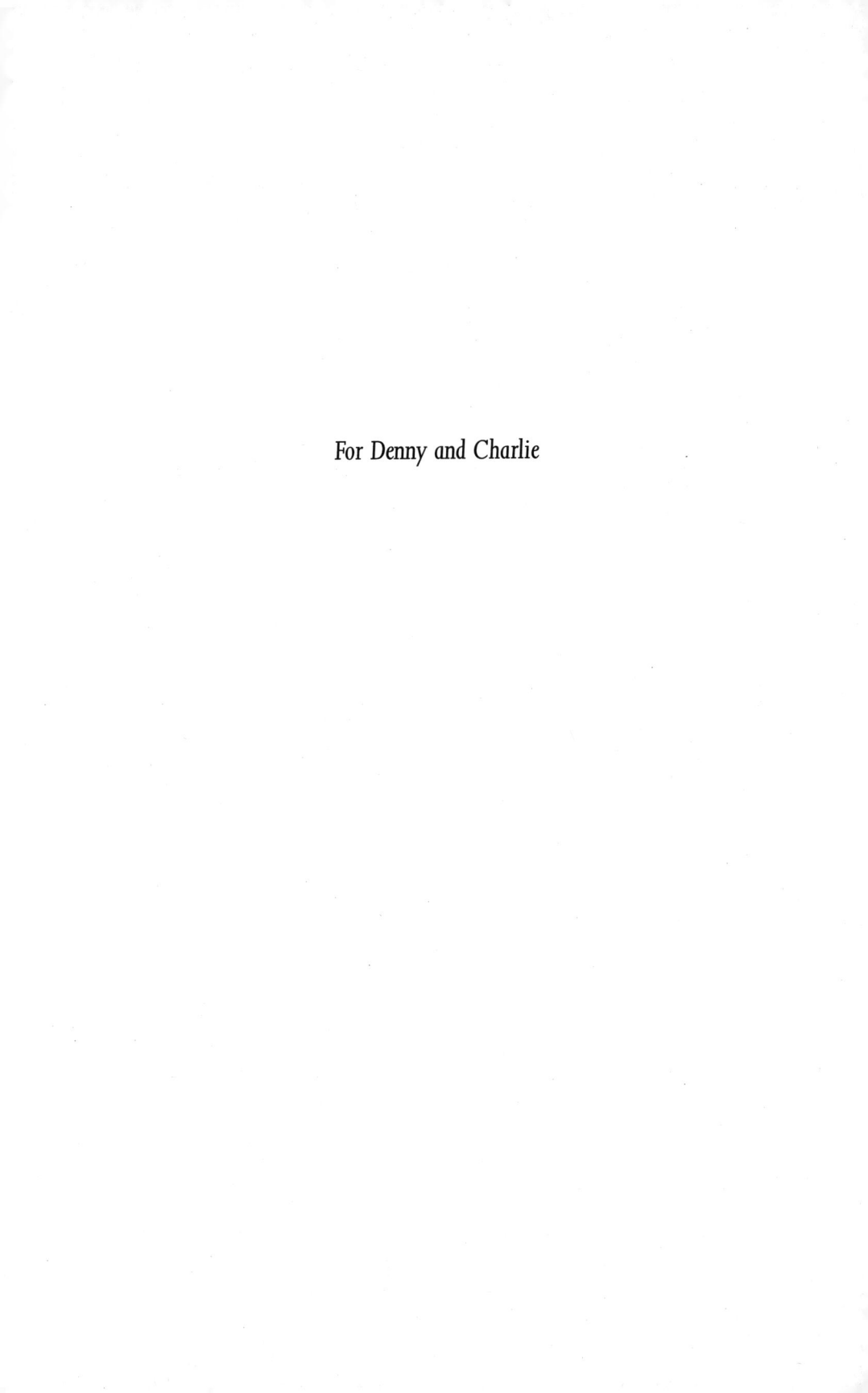

# Contents

Incantation     11

## I

Mapping the Human Genome     15
Birth     16
Male Taken from Female     17
Sex and Breakfast     18
Rich with Desire     20
The Girl/The Girlie Magazine     21
Fear of Intelligence     22
Blood in the Water     24
Remembering the Delivery Room,
     Children's Hospital     25

## II

Knowing     29
Ithaca. The Seaward Wife     30
Olivia: The Spiral between Men and Women     32
Flu, Spring Rain, and You     33
October Mother     34
Contagious Magic     36
Scary Warmth     38
The Red Thread     40
Wildness Breaking In     42
Bicycling     44
Leda, to the Black Swan     46

## III

Calf Born in Snow     49
Secrets at My Uncle's House     50
Miss Western Auto     54

| | |
|---|---|
| Mt. Bethany Cedar | 56 |
| My Uncle's Study | 58 |
| Blue Coals | 60 |
| Blessing | 61 |
| Late in the Day | 62 |

## IV

| | |
|---|---|
| Thin Air | 67 |
| Rink | 68 |
| September Air | 69 |
| The Feel of Her Heart | 70 |
| After the Argument | 72 |
| Monument Water | 74 |
| Contagion | 75 |
| City Like an Advent Calendar | 76 |
| Flesh and Sanity | 78 |
| | |
| Notes | 79 |

## Incantation

Step onto the deck. Push off.
This vessel is made of intelligence—
yours and mine—the stuff we have
whittled back to a poor imitation,
to fragments measured on tests.
Put back what the body knows,
return soul to bone, wrap mind
in its scarlet-cloaked case, feel
ideas form. You have only
to step aboard to shed your old life.

I

# Mapping the Human Genome

A trail is being blazed to the people who preceded us,
whose troubling nucleotides we so clearly
contain. Probably, nothing could have changed
my ancestor McKay's blue eyes or prevented him,
that dark night in the woods, from ravishing
the Senedo girl who became our forebear here.

What made him live to be 90 and
his brother only 18 was luck.
Other families were more adaptable, tough.
Some of their men, like Meriwether Lewis,
survived by learning to eat dog meat
and to "prefer it vastly to lean venison or elk."

Lewis's map was huge. Open it out
on the library table, and you can see the point
at which British place names give way,
leading to Snake River, Bitterroot Mountains,
Clearwater—names that seem part of the earth,
integral as veins carrying sustenance through.

Today's trailblazers map us.
Ancient questions arise, but in a language
scientists do not understand. Their calipers
can't reach the lost knowledge running in us
like a river. It turns, spurls, and spits uncharted
currents—so close, so fierce—just under the bone.

# Birth

Tulips blaze yellow in the vase
as my son bursts in from school—
his fifth-grade science lesson
glistening in his eyes. "We saw
a foetus in a jar," he says, and

"His birthday was the same
as mine. I could have been
in that jar. He could have
been standing there, looking at *me*."

On the table behind him, a petal
is missing from one of the tulips, leaving
a thin glimpse of stamen—such as
the openings we get sometimes—the one
my son slipped through today, blooming.

## Male Taken from Female

He was torn from her thigh, that first man in Eden—
bone splintered skin, formed into sinews, tendons
of him—but she rose unharmed and walked
through fields, sunlight running down her shoulders
and hair like electricity. Even before the sixth day,
her spirit lived, for her energy has always been. Winds
moved with her over earth and fields. Trees dropped
their succulence into her hands, each fruit carrying its
own seed within. Small animals, also, rose up in this time
for her touch. Her right hand stroked the mane
of a black mare that shivered its pleasure beside her.

This first being came from water. With each footfall,
she felt the rough-textured earth, the early surfaces
of land. And even before he was formed, man
lived within her—took shape in Eden to help her.
When he sprang from her thigh, rolled over and stood,
she brushed twigs from his hair, dirt from his legs—
as if he were a large child in her care. Speechless,
he would find words to praise her. Already, he felt
the fierce longing to return to her steady certainty,
squatted strength. So it was then and is now—this
story kept from you, a secret you have always known.

## Sex and Breakfast

Smelling of pancakes and sex, she stands
at the stove cooking breakfast. Her husband
wants the woman at work, but comes
home to her every night, the sensible choice.

Butter skitters and pops. When she reduces
the flame, a green mantis climbs to the sill,
turning its triangular head this way and that,
eyes like beads of dark water on the hypotenuse.

Creepy. The creature could crawl to the stove's
glistening surface, touch her with the seamy leaf
of itself, but instead, it crunches the remains
of a fly in foreshortened arms—as if

it had gnawed off its hands in an error
of passion. A ravening hunger ignited her
husband that morning. They tried many ways
to extinguish the picture that flared up between them

like flaming starter fluid recklessly applied. With a towel,
she brushes the mantis from sill to floor and sweeps
it outside, carries their breakfast to the porch.
Her husband finds chairs, cushions, cloth napkins.

They settle at last in sunlight, over fast-cooling food,
loving again the outdoors, themselves, even insects,
the comforts of Sunday—newspapers, rumors, crosswords
revised. She opens her legs slightly, wearing

nothing beneath. Like a school boy, he watches
as she works the puzzle, shifting now and then.
He could stare forever at that mystery,
the way a man does, never getting enough.

# Rich with Desire

We wake in the room I grew up in,
birds chirping summer outside,
the child of our bodies thrumming
his delight, kicking small feet,
waving flexed arms like wings
in the crib that was mine—just
as this bed was mine and still holds
the shape of my girlish body
before the fevered intrusions of love.
Hold me then, husband,
in this protected place, rich
with lust, as we turn and turn
in the covers, trespassing through time.

# The Girl/The Girlie Magazine

*Who is the third who walks always beside you?*
                            —T. S. Eliot

She is in full color,
her legs splayed
on a page glossy as any
displaying dolls
in Sears' Christmas book.
She's been creased at the crotch
and shoved under the front seat
of my father's Buick,
which it's my job to clean.

To look at her is better than to be her—
she with her flume exposed,
her steamy regions laid open.
Does my father read entrails?
What does he see?

I did not want to be her,
but to view her.
Viewer—controller
of pitted extremes,
of the animal slouching eastward,
"moving its slow thighs."

Now—
sometimes now—
in the silky moonlight
as your hand strokes my thigh,
if the bed seems cold or I distant,
it is this: I am the third watching,
coolly touching finger to tongue,
turning the slick, creased page.

# Fear of Intelligence

*For Ann*

When you took yourself to school
in the yellow-bright September sun
(prickly as a whiskered kiss on your skin)
and walked into the dark building filled
with chalky smells and smudged boards
and sat in a strange desk that swallowed
your summer without even a burp:

How was it then, to be the smartest
kid, the one in the first row who
spelled "nephew" and "xylophone,"
and later the new kid came like
a cold blast from the northeast,
full of "precocity" and "promise"—
as the teachers whispered?

How was it to be a little girl sitting
on the stoop at recess, wanting to cut
through the fog that kept you from saying to him,
"Just because I'm rural—doesn't mean I'm
stupid"—and to feel your classmates' anger
crowd around your accurate answers—
and to be smarter than the boys?

And then to go to college, make a "B" on a test
you should have aced and doubt not
the teacher, the questions, the school, but
yourself? And suppose you met someone
smarter than you: who had not just better
memory, math or music skills, facility
with language, artistic talent—but all of these?

And what if you married him,
your claim to importance disabled
like a broken clamp—this man rising up
before you expecting to be right? And
years later, to learn you were smarter—
your jaw like a revolver chamber hanging open,
emptied, nothing to back it up—
and now, too late, you're out of love
and struggling with the elements
of a puzzle, the last pieces always lost—
but finally just to leave them there?

*Oh September sun, come again. Bring*
*the whiskered kiss, the long yellow days*
*and tall shadows, pencils, lockers in the hall,*
*students doing lessons.* A rupture
in your spirit seals, as you,
drink mystery from the apple core,
turn loamy earth, smell burning leaves—
anchored by the smallest thing it takes
to teach you now, to hold you here.

# Blood in the Water

The Old Mother's hands fetch
into my body the rhythm of beads
being strung, and by the Shenandoah,
I can feel her spirit run in the green
purling water. A boy on the bank
swings out from an oak and drops
like a stone, thunk-splash. Nearby,
the brown raft lifts and sinks. Spraying
drops smell river-clean, releasing memories
of married summer days when the monster
of our separate selves came up—that dark
underside waiting like a sinker
on the floor till it hooked my throat,
and I jerked toward death, then freedom.

# Remembering the Delivery Room, Children's Hospital

This bright, sterile room is not what
I want for your birth. It mocks the old fires
within—odors of lichen and earth.

The hot fist of family history has me
in its grip, grasping and squeezing.
Pain, that clangorous train, whizzes through—

till another barrels toward me. Frayed cords
of six generations snap. You split the wet hemi-
spheres between us, ocean salt drenching the sheet.

I swear the Old Mother enters: Senedo
apparition in the doorway, coming
to my side. Her hand flattens beneath me.

*They'll tell you to push,*
*she whispers, but don't listen.*
*Mine is the hand you must trust.*

The hum of her blood sings you
to me. Your cry is but a soft complaint
to the world you will love fist-to-mouth,

savoring its taste, mysteries
of the Blue Ridge in your fingers,
song of red hope in your throat.

# II

*In time, and with water, everything changes.*
— Leonardo da Vinci

# Knowing

Evie smiles in pain and hope, knowing she nailed
him, even if he mashed her face for it—his tongue
tied in knots before her right words. Cheek scraped,
she rests briefly in the corner. Soon she must lie:
say she ran into a door or fell from a chair.

Perhaps she could leave, but the cloud
descends—a gray uselessness that keeps her
from moving. There will be days of sweetness
ahead: apologies, roses. Things could change.

She opens the back door to the smell of damp
earth after rain and feels her cheek sting. Gingko fans
flip here and there. Wind whistles down the hollow
of the moment, molding her skirt to her legs.

*He won't change,* she thinks. *They were right. But more
than that: neither will I.* Maps for change spread
through her body. She will need money to safeguard
what is hers, a place to stay—at least a roof and door—plywood
to cover windows, other things that break loose in a storm.

## Ithaca. The Seaward Wife

I have grown brown in the sun's eye,
with this little black-haired boy clinging
to my arm, hugging my waist with
his scratched legs. We watch

daily for the sight of his father's sails—
or for some off-shore vision of the man who
fights with the world—but more with himself—
to turn the bow of his ship toward home.

You ask why he stayed away so long—
all against his will? I who know him best,
know the dark corners of his heart,
the clashing rocks he daily sails through.

Whirling, he fights for a prize
(to save his life?) to find some ease, for he
would sooner risk life and limb fighting
Trojans and one-eyed monsters

than endure the closest moments of the marriage
bed. That much happiness is not natural for us,
for in a moment we could wash over the edge
of the world and rock in blissful darkness there.

"A cardboard faithful wife" the story
paints me, but how could I know his secret
heart, had I not fought the selfsame foes?
They also come to a woman young, alive, alone.

I confide: in dreams he came here in disguise, and
I slept with men who seemed like him—who in the
deepest night revealed his scar. We were strange
lovers in that time. Our mirror selves continue yet.

# Olivia: The Spiral between Men and Women

To the men whose bodies lied when
they pushed into me, lovers who
thought my love was free and disposable
as diapers of the baby they did not
care if they left with me—as if their
most intimate acts had no consequence.

A man like that is without power;
has not learned to take it up, so that
when he marries his body to a woman
in the dark, he becomes like an amputee—
with part of himself cut away—or a brain-
empty being thrashing around in a fit
of misunderstanding of who he is and why
anything he does with his body matters.

I have done the same thing, myself:
taken my clothes off for a man
I did not love, as if that most revealing act
were just a pill to take to feel better—
or a convenience, like using a doormat
to get the caked mud off my shoes
before entering another reality.

But the doorway is dark. It leads to
the soul, where the helix between men
and women exists, where Yum, the whirl-
wind spirit with full range of motion, raises
the circle of life toward calm. In this place
of spiral and scent, there are only two ways
to travel. Let yours be the way leading up.

# Flu, Spring Rain, and You

Lying in bed, flu-bogged,
I wonder what mean quirk of fate
makes my body cry out
for the muscle and contour of yours
two years after our divorce
and one year into my new love.

I'm too weak for anything but need,
and need you I do. Though you're
in California and I'm with someone
new, the vines of our marriage
are bound up in my veins
like a virus green and climbing,

making my body crave comforts
from a marriage that continues
like a stump in the forest—
dead—except for a few green
sprigs, persistent at weakest
moments in spring rain.

# October Mother

*for my mother's mother*

Bound like baling twine by timeless seasons, she moves
overripe through Indian summer, swell-bellied, slow,
touching October's clarity with mellow fingers, tracing
charcoal limbs against the chill, orange sky.

I've eight like you, spasmic child inside—
you who slow my winding down,
coming unannounced to claim my body
as your sprouting ground. What right
have you?

More right, perhaps, than all the rest
who walked through my body to their birth,
pulling down my brittle bones,
kicking ribs aside, residing
where you are now, inside.

In all eight chances,
I missed the child I sought.
Like a shell, I held them without hope.
At first, I tried to mold them
with names like Stella, Honor,
Lewis, Jeremiah.
They shoved aside these sounds
like useless, membraned shards.
Now whole, now free,
they spurned me.

But you, frantic child, late intrusion,
last sweet berry of the season,
with your insistent conjurings of my youth,
kicking at your cord, making me believe
I'm twenty, instead of forty-four.
Our labor will be swift.
Ripe melons fall easy from the vine.
(I even doubt that I will bleed.)
Your name will be no incantation—
just autumnal syllables softly combined;
your cry will be a blaze of glory;
your birth, the only magic that I need.

## Contagious Magic

Standing outside in the spring night
under a wide Washington moon—
away from the party voices drifting out . . .
my husband and our lawyer friends
go on about the need for reason,
as if it were a forgotten deity,
and they, its only acolytes.

"We can't curtail First Amendment
rights," a man's voice . . ."censor film
and TV. . . . sex, violence regrettable, BUT. . . ."
In the silver-blue light, a black Lab
thunders across the yard trying
to mount the neighbor's Golden.
His color blends with the night,
till jerking motions, trembling
haunches give him away
at the driveway's edge.

As I turn, the ash tree's
lowest branch snags my hair.
Its slight sting makes me stop.
In moonlight, the tree seems alive.
Its trunk has a woman's belly—
and above: two mounds, symmetrical
as breasts. I place my hand
between the mounds, hoping
to feel a heart beating there.

Tonight, I could free any spirit
in that tree. Am I mad or drunk
sipping the last Zinfandel? I smash
the glass on slate. If the tree
seems alive and I bold, the night is
that warm; the stakes, that high.

## Scary Warmth

Windows light up like opening eyes
as I finish the chores,
 enter the kitchen
to shed coat and gloves,
pick up a pumpkin,
and sharpen a knife to gut it.

I'm home briefly after divorce,
on the evening that spirits
come in from the fields
seeking hearth fires.
A sinister energy runs
through us, as blood claims revive.

Fiber and seeds cling to my fingers.
"Cut teeth," my brother orders.
"Make him scary."
"No, don't," the children argue.
"Find a candle," I tell my sister.
(She's stealing my land.)

When I seat the candle, and it falls,
Brother begins his tirade:
"Stupid. You don't
know what you're doing!"
The eyes flame up,
flicker forward,

as if some wicked life returned,
igniting the black hills of Scotland
where our ancestors burned fern,
thorn, and stubble
to drive back the cold.

Their bickering strength continues
in the viscous threads that bind us.
When I turn the carved face to the window,
it glows a twisted warning.
The faulty grin falters, then hovers . . .
the great hollow head holds our heat.

# The Red Thread

*Atropos, Clotho,* and *Lachesis*

What Goddess of Scissors
  made us mother and daughter?
  What sheer necessity,
  wove her thread into mine?

What Goddess of Cloth
  clutched my hair,
  shoved me under the treadle
  of a woman who lives by rules
  and sprigs of jasmine?

What Goddess of Length
  made me try to be like her:
  stitching, snipping, making quilts?
  Even today I sleep under her
  Double Wedding Ring—

A quilt so thin it could not warm me,
  except in lilac light
  or before the bright, crackling heat
  of her unyielding hearth.

Some kind of snarled love
  tries to leap out between us,
  over embankments
  like a violet budding in rock.

Leaving this morning,
    I lift from her hands a covered bowl—
    raspberries from the garden—
    "Take them," she says.
    "I picked them for you."

## Wildness Breaking In

Within me, the unlimited plow, farmlands,
      and the English settler's greed,
      the low meanness of the moralist preacher,

And in me, the pocked city streets, odors
      wafting from bakeries, tawdry
      nightclubs and P Street Beaches, the rock-ridden
      park—its foliage green down the city's red throat—
      frail jonquils on hillsides trembling—the jay's sharp call.

Within me a bureaucracy working—its windows
      permanently sealed, long rows of PCs humming,
      rumors of murders with anger and without—
      the cold seizing of life.

And, in me the rending shriek that today splits the dull hum
      of work, the terrible wrenching gut-cry of the woman
      whose son was shot, the dropped phone and stunned
      stillness among us, waves of anger and pain cracking open. . . .

Rain smashing against glass—a wildness
      breaking in, its thundering masculinity—
      the taking without permission in the heat
      of day, with only a promise of cool.

Then the slowing down,
>	the whirring and clogging machinery
>	chugging the District to a stop, sirens
>	shooting through consciousness like a drug
>	in the veins. Rain plundering down, setting
>	the bloodroot throbbing in the vacant lot.

We watch from windows or street corners,
>	with protection—without—hunkering
>	down, then the new thrust: to know ourselves
>	all brothers—mysterious, frightening brothers—
>	for the blood ties that hold us, bind us.
>	We are not safe.

# Bicycling

The medical student next door rides home on the Gitane he took to
New Zealand last year unaware
as he passes the bayberry bush that his wife stood there hours earlier
leaning her slender body toward
a bearded man, an intern, who looked down at her as if he did not
see restraint like a capital "R"

on her breast or the wind caressing her legs as she took his words
into her mouth—
turning them this way and that. The intern smiled awkwardly wishing
to have the words back.
Watching her speak, he considered asking, "May I have them again?"
But that made no sense.

He could think
of nothing to say—he who was perhaps smarter than her husband
Rob—who by all counts was odd—
willing to leave school for six months in his third year and bicycle
with his wife around an island,
the seasons of which were exactly backward.

Watching her shoulders, he could see lamb's wool, rugged
green hillsides, and kelp.
And there was something about her hair, so straight and glossy,
which, if let down
would become a curtain he might lift and part to step into
a private room

where she and her husband slept. He grew tired imagining them
riding many bicycles
uphill. ". . . come to dinner sometime," she was saying, and taken by
surprise, he nodded, like a distant older relative kindly included.

As she turned to go, he knew he'd lost ground, ground he replaced
rapidly enough
at the hospital where he flipped through the epileptic's chart, ordered
Tegretol, q.i.d., where he strolled the corridors, stethoscope still
round his neck, chatting with nurses.

Later, in ER, as he bathed the eyes of a child and answered the parents'
questions, soberly,
with professional detachment, he glimpsed Rob passing by on his
way to the lot, where, no doubt
Rob would unlock the Gitane, smile as if medicine were incidental,
lift its featherweight up,
and begin pumping effortlessly home.

## Leda, to the Black Swan

Like a gloved thief, you came
to my chamber this morning, fingering
the particulars of light on the bed,
turning back the sheet to vulnerable skin.

Soft down, then feathers sprouted
from your body as you pulled me outside, spread
your great wings to transport us.
When we lifted off, with a loud blundering motion,

your webbed claws could have drawn blood
from my waist or punctured my side,
but you held me slipping and turning
above garrets, skylights. Even in faint light,

I could see teal and crimson wink
from your ebony feathers, oh wise
and treacherous one. The trip out of here
is through rain that could drown or baptize.

Below us, workers pursue their cautious concerns,
but my arms extend. The pure exuberance
of flight is in me. No wonder I fear you.
No wonder I run from/approach you with equal speed.

# III

*. . . carry fire to the next tribal town, for the renewal of spirit.*
—Joy Harjo, *A Map to the Next World*

# Calf Born in Snow

I can still hear the loud moan
in my grandfather's kitchen,
where the woodstove was open
for the failing fire's warmth, and
on the oven door, wrapped
in an old quilt, lay the new Charolais calf—
a twin that survived its snowy birth
that morning, though its brother died—
both of them the color of muddy snow,
this one too weak to stand.

We tried to feed him his mother's milk,
but he seemed to forget he was eating
and slept, so that by ten that night, when
he raised his head suddenly, making
a loud maa-a-a-a sound, I could scarcely
believe it. "He's getting better!"
Dad put his hand on my shoulder.
 "Quiet. He's dying," was all he said—
old knowledge, deep as the Blue Mountains.
Still, I'd witnessed that final, wonderful
rallying, as if every ounce of life pulled
together to raise the calf's head,
to leave his sound so indelibly there.

# Secrets at My Uncle's House

### I.
I learned from you the elegance of proof,
complex math, and my own inadequacies,
that imagination steals energy from the real world—
and even memory, so tidy and selective,
can be brutal in its sameness from which
the density of touch is vanished,
from which completion is barred,
as it is for the buck leaping at the fence
or the puzzle always being worked on your table.

I have come here, Uncle, for my sanity
that it might stabilize like an object in your room—
like the fox skull you found in a field and baked
till the spiders ran out. If there is any wisdom,
it is in collections such as these,
in the clutter of your nests and shells,
in the gargoyle or geode that waits
to be taken up and turned in the hand
as if some lesson were in it—a clue
to the unfocused excitement it provokes.

Or wisdom might grow from movement,
from the circular sweep of your arm
as you lean over the conch shell puzzle
searching for the shape you must have,
while I rest my cheek on the smooth
leather chair (that sits on the worn rug
slightly off-square) and gaze at the objects
everywhere on ledges: mock-ups, old prints,
open books. It is evening and the curtains
are open. At the window your telescope slants
toward the North Star, as if this house were
a navigable craft, and you were to take her home.

## II.

For breakfast, Mrs. Bailey prepares
your barley—without exception—
the thin milk, a kind of liquid peace
to be spooned into one's mouth.
She does not know that your father
made this table of dark cherry, tooled
its legs, or that when the leaf
is extended, the leg pulled forward,
it opens into other rooms, those
of your childhood and mine—
and further back to grandfathers before
us, to the one who came in 1780 to survey
west of the Blue Ridge, but stayed that first
winter on the mountain with a Senedo woman
and staked his claim. Our dark grandmother
was not mentioned until you told the story:
She lay her body against his in the bitter wind
and rain. When spring came, she taught him
what Europe forgot. Guiding his fingers
with hers, she helped him fashion a bow.

### III.

To make a bow, choose a small tree,
three handspans in girth. Ask permission.
If not given, move on. When you sense
acceptance, begin with a flint knife.
Make a groove in the trunk
the width of your two fingers,
and another groove six handspans above it.
Cut out a long strip between them,
and season the strip a full year;
carve into a graceful bow.
Wipe gently with bear grease,
and string with sinews of deer.
Before the bow bends to your hand
or learns the strength of your pull,
honor its beauty, the speed of the bear
and deer, the skyward lift of the tree.
No one will take it from you.

## Miss Western Auto

The past jumps forward from inside the lit viewer
when Dan shows me the 3-D photo of Elly
and me in strapless gowns standing beside
the fir tree in Granddad's yard, waiting
for the Field Day parade. Our creamy
shoulders and bright looks startle me.

Dan says he could almost
step into the picture, taken
with my uncle's Revere camera,
and walk between those girls frozen
in time on the third Saturday in August
as they wait for the float to carry them away.

The white clapboard house is the same.
Even the light in the yard is the right
golden hue for boarding the float
with my friend. As we ride into town,
wave, throw candy to children,
I am learning the power of beauty.

At the temporary stage, guards
from the Junior Order offer their arms,
present us with blue-tinted carnations
(which we pin on) and numbers
we carry before us like fans.

My uncles, once so safe and protective,
slip into the crowd, joining men who
look us up and down like items at auction
requiring a bid. *What happened—they've changed?*
a small voice in me cries as the program begins.

Rivulets of sweat run down my temples
and cleavage. "Miss Western Auto," my
banner says, and though it scratches, I
like it, for it means I am one of the chosen.

Called back before the judges,
I try to guess what they see. The winner
is named, and suddenly, the special attention
is all gone. I become an awkward girl,
whose hair is too short and straight,
whose legs are too long.

Dan complains we'll be late,
so I put down the past to dress in red,
with strappy pumps, glittering earrings:
today's look. Still, the aura
of that day returns when a man
jumps up, holds my chair.

I wonder at the pageantry of it,
the distance between viewer
and viewed, the binocular nature
of vision that allows our two eyes
to see separately, but blend
completely for depth.

## Mt. Bethany Cedar

Sunday morning, honeysuckle lyrics lurk
in the sweet throat of my father, as he sings
"Abide with Me," his voice blending with
the bass and tenor of men eager
to get through this ordeal and go out front
for a smoke. Rubbing thorn-scratched knuckles,
Dad folds down his hymnal to the bench.

"What hath God wrought?" Reverend Whitaker
asks the ceiling. My two-year-old brother twists
sideways, drops his rear off the bench, while
Sis tucks her pink dress under plump legs
and points black patent toes toward me.
Dad ponders the motor grease
that did not clean from his nails.

I have already left them—drifted out
the window to stand under dogwood blossoms—
the stained edge of their petals
like pinched violence—drifting further still,
over church roads, near ringing fields
where soon bee hums will rise from clover,
and I will be free of battering pulpits, hackling
hearts of a congregation driving the fear
of life in like a carpenter's nail.

"And ye generation of vipers,
how can ye escape the damnation of hell?"
Oh, forget this eternal damnation,
I want to tell them. Listen instead
to the leaf music calling your names
from the trees, winding its way over creek beds,
the calming breath of the ancients is in it—
they who watched over us, when we
did not watch over ourselves;
even before your time and mine.

## My Uncle's Study

The classics shelved, bound in leather,
books with hidden drawings on the fore edges . . .
here, ideas almost seep through the seams.
Minds come down from the shelf:
Homer's muscular thought moves like waves
with undercurrents felt only at a distance.
Plato's clipped thought is all parallel lines, angles.
Like Kant, Duns Scotus appears. Tall and
quick, the Celt made verbal mazes
so cleverly that when I believe I am out,
Scotus himself, with a smirk, blocks my path.

Uncle, I loved the glistening spine of your
thought: its hooklike projections and spikes.
Invertebrate thought does not move me: it is
the pattern of my own mind. In this room
that looks to the sea, imagination can fly
to the edge of the world, swim there with dragons.
Leaning on your fluffed pillows, we sip
Courvoisier warmed to the tongue. Restraint
(that black arrow) appears only briefly, rarely
hitting the mark. "No act of will can save us
the trouble of self-destruction," you once said.

Uncle, my brother might love men. The discovery
could finger its way over toys left in the chest.
I remember his hands. When did it start? If love
is a humiliation, a humbling, perhaps it is less so
with the same sex. So much wordless perception
lives in the sexual body. When one looks out,
craving a body like one's own, is that
full acceptance of the self as complete?

Seductive thought. No wonder the ancients
enforced logic against unruly ideas. In this room,
answers become possibilities, phantom
philosophies grow in your petri dish study.
Tonight, pressing my eye to the telescope
brings the North Star closer, as if the Big Dipper
could pull things together under it, though
I still want the stars you once
showed me to be diamonds, winking.

# Blue Coals

"Why didn't they bow down?" I wanted
to know about Shadrach, Meshach,
Abed-nego. "Because they were honorable,"
Dad said, and when Nebuchadnezzar cast them
into the furnace, they still did not bow down,
but walked through the fire unsinged
with no smell of burning about them.

They were stoic like Dad, who lies
in his bed—a father who smacked me
so I would be good. But what does
that matter now as he gives away life
to the dark fist drumming him down?
*Stand up! Refuse,* I want to say, but this
is no Bible story, no fable for children.

His eyes—once fierce-blue—are blunted
and dull, and the bones of his body, mere racks
for draped flesh. In three days, he'll be gone.
When the funeral comes, we are given
a plastic box full of ashes, chunks of bone,
and I can't let it go. "Dad, you must tell me . . ."
("Shush," they say, "Quiet.")

*You must tell me . . . Does the body move*
*in such heat? When the flames warmed*
*your poor cold flesh, did the muscles*
*of your arms reach out? Did you*
*stand up, once again, then?*
*In the depths of the fire,*
*did your eyes seize life?*

# Blessing

*For a great-great-grandfather*

In from the field at noon,
Grandfather was obliged
to put on a suit coat
to come to Grandmother's table.
He'd sweat rivulets receiving
the green beans and corn,
iced tea, Thy bounty, Lord.
When he stood up, coat soiled,
she'd turn away—a marrow
of demand in those perfect
cheekbones. Then, back
with the applesauce cake,
she'd pause by his chair—
a hint of spice about her.

## Late in the Day

We continue our grievances
at dinner: the short one is teased,
the thin one maligned, rivalries

rekindled, grown children disowned.
The holiday meal nearly ended, we abandon
turkey bone and gristle, cranberry sauce

sweet and bitter as blood,
and surrender one by one to the children
urging us out to play aerobie.

My son and ex-husband have gone to new
families. Only my brother, sister and children,
and the sturdy man I now love

stand with me in the lengthening light
to toss the plastic ring
that rises as if to go over the sun,

though it glides up in a slow loop only—
and down, passing from hand to hand.
The brother who has tormented me

tosses carefully now, so that I will catch
and throw to the child between us,
or to my sister who, with her great bulk,

hoards all that she has lost, yet
lumbers to catch the ring, as the circle
widens like a ripple or shrinks

to hold something we've never known—
how to be together without rancor—
as if life could be just this easy,

and the family we are given by birth (or by choice)
is the right one for us—the only one—
and this life, this one life, is enough.

IV

# Thin Air

On the first day of flight, Orville Wright carried
a small leather journal in his pocket to record
wind speed: "over 20 miles" and Wilbur's plane
flying "852 feet" in less than a minute.
Today, Dan and I, carrying hang-gliders
on our backs, climb Jockey's Ridge—
a huge dune near their site.
Wings, heavy as a cumbersome past, teeter
on my shoulders. When I try to run fast,
my feet sink in sand, but then, almost magically,
the wing-weight lifts, and I glide over beach sand
dotted with scrubs and gulls. Awed by the view,
I steer too sharply and crash, denting the ground
and my arm. Dan helps me up, but like Wilbur,
I just want more—more time when flight lifts
me out of the usual world into sumptuous suspension,
where air can support a winged machine,
and nothing twists such a miracle off course or
shoots down the trust it takes to hold it up.

# Rink

Mark's muscles moved, taut, tanned—a shirtless man
laying brick. At 12, I hardly knew what stirred me
to watch for hours: his trowel, flick of wrist,
and the way he shoveled just the right measure
of sand to mix with water and cement. He taught classics,
English. "Best-educated bricklayer in the county,"
my father said. Mark asked if I knew gray-eyed Athena,
Odysseus's guardian, or Persephone, who gathered flowers,
as I liked to do. He used it all: education, muscles,
lean precision building a chimney for our house.
His muscles slipped and glided, as he mixed
mortar, smoothed it to grainy glue. Then one night
at the skating rink, I saw him as I laced my skates,
began the long oval sweep. He leapt and spun
in the center, skated backward toward me—
as if, using skill enough and speed, he might
do a twist-turn-leap and break the quick distance
between us, before he closed in, circled,
flipped my hair once, skated on.

# September Air

Traces of helium, xenon, even krypton are in it. Air is only
1/5 oxygen, the stuff our body needs to nourish blood, fund
thought, help wounds heal. We pull air in climbing hills,
running 10-Ks, leaping or diving—but stop right there
and simply breathe. This afternoon in bed with you,
I breathe slowly—our bodies still warm and
disheveled from love. The air seems almost
conjurable, as if we could bring into view
the substance that holds the tiny particles
falling so leisurely in slant light that
gravity seems suspended, and they,
like us, lift out of the ordinary
for a moment and show
themselves in bright
September light,
before sinking
again from
view.

## The Feel of Her Heart

The surgeon on the plane explains that he opens a chest the way earth
is turned in the spring by a farmer plowing near rock.
Though the task is complex, its purpose is plain:
to repair the infant heart
that seizes and scurries like a leaf in wind—
blood leaking like water.

Beside him, I imagine a rainbow of sudsy water
arcing over his hands as he scrubs earth
crescents from his nails. A farmer at heart,
he leaves his garden at dawn, forgetting the rocks
and worm-riddled soil to lean over a plain
tub in a sterile room that admits no sun or wind.

Here, he considers the gust in his patient's chest, a fickle wind
trouncing her heart
that weighs like a rock
in her chest, while out in the hall, her father drinks water
from a cup, asking *Is this my daughter's last day on earth?*
The doctor, to steady himself, imagines a plain—

no fences or barriers occlude this plain
or block his work on the delicate heart,
(small as a hen's egg) as he lifts it, blood shunting like water
through tubes to machines. Her heart's wind
stilled, the body submits, just as earth
submits to rain pummeling its cliffs and rocks.

The heart's blue membrane, slick as wet rock,
frightens the surgeon. Creek beds of childhood (water
distorting his wading footstep) appear; the winds
threaten to drown him. It's plain,
something like earth
slips from beneath his feet as he massages her heart

until, on the screen, a break point of heart-
beat appears, plain
evidence that life flows again like water
encountering no rock.
She twitches. The flicker of life leaps up, as if fanned by wind,
and the girl-child returns to her future on earth.

At noon, the doctor departs. His plane lifts from earth
on benevolent winds. As he unwinds, sipping scotch on the rocks,
the feel of her heart slowly fades from his palm; ice cubes melt into water.

## After the Argument

### I

If I could capture the moon, I would
bring it to your cottage whole, wrapped
in lace underclothes—its pure light pooling
on the sheets where we used to lie. In your sleep,
dreaming of mandarins and ginger, you would
turn in the light and smile, your cinnamon
hair tangled in a silver-smudged glow.

And, if I could hold all our days, pull back
the curtains that slouch and slump on the floor
to see ahead, I'd tell you honestly, I do not
understand the love you give me.
Is there nothing you would keep back?

### II

I did not guess you'd come to me, red hair
turning white, curly locks and beard, tall,
big of belly, dripping from the sea. Nor did I
know you pulled its lower depths with you—
that all your life, you'd crashed within its storms.

On land, your caring broke surface in finest seams,
cool mists against the sunburnt heat.
You came into my landlocked life
like a Norwegian ship captain ridden by a fly–
your changing face: clouds across the Sea Force.

In loving you, my shell broke loose. I was vulnerable
as a sea creature at low tide—and flourished there.
So many times you swept us past my limits. I took
your daughters to my heart; your son's arrogance,
I forgave; I had such hunger for your taste.

### III

Now, at day's end, driving down K Street toward a moon
that squats hugely on the horizon–sweet moon
of warm butter, watching me approach as if inviting my car
to arc from street to sky to cross over the distance
and wreckage between us—I can almost hear the song
you sang: "All I need is the air that I breathe and
to love you. . . ." and hearing, hope there is a way.

# Monument Water

*. . . in the long journey ahead of you . . . your wolf will have become
another wolf, your sister a different sister . . . [in] the city where memory
is traded at every solstice and at every equinox.*
          — Italo Calvino, *Invisible Cities*

Hungry for what makes a life work, I want to remove
the water's reflections, stop the shifting shapes, sieve out
clutter, and find what's hidden beneath, but nothing there
could reveal as much as this monument water, holding
buildings and people together after a summer shimmer of rain.

The artists I've met this week dance inside me.
Their histories—mysteries of transformation—mix
with my own, here at the reflecting pool, where
clouds explode into myth. Artemis, Psyche, Eros
float, tangle, make love, give shape to our fates.

But at the Vietnam wall, human stories unfold. The surface
captures sky and ground, giving it back again with only fragments
of clouds—too small for the muscle of myth to emerge. Reflected
from behind me, three boys play tag. They run stumbling
toward their Mom, laughing as they vanish in the stone.

# Contagion

*Pulling to the self that which destroys: wiping*
*up the simplest viral start with bare hands,*
the young blondes and brunettes in the 1930s photo
kneel in house dresses to clean the marble
steps of the Library of Congress. All of them,
slim and maternal, so close to the dirt,
wiping the gray-fouled stone this way and that
by hand, with large, soft cloths.

I wish I could walk up those stairs, cleaned
by women in flowered dresses, wiped
with their hands, but today, masked workers
bring loud machines and bristled polishers,
and women no longer kneel for such work
(nor would I want them to, nor would I like to),
yet today something in me wishes for them,
for my foot to touch the cleanliness of that labor.

# City Like an Advent Calendar

It begins when Union Station's massive
green wreaths announce the season, and
I pass them to drive up North Capitol on
the gray, muscular streets of Washington
past the Rehab Hospital's lit window, where
Dan's mother recuperated from her stroke,
and then on into Takoma Park where carolers
carry candles on the street, and
the Black Box Theater window opens
onto cast members scurrying to the stage
for the play I directed six years ago, and,
now when I stop at the Branch Library,
my dear friend, who, though we are very
different, looks up and says, "Damn,
it's good to see you," and the handful of poets
there for the reading open their presents afterward.

When Dan drives us back to the Hill,
down Wisconsin Avenue, I see not the restaurant
that exists, but the Zebra Room that was once
near the Zoo, and behind the mind's Advent window,
even the sad pandas that couldn't conceive
continuing as if they were there.

At the National Cathedral, the gargoyle
Anne's boyfriend carved of her with her tongue
sticking out snarls from a corner, a reminder
of the time she resigned her job
with Sharon Karol, who is blind.
Though I passed Sharon in the hallway today,
she was quiet. This bright, feisty woman,
who had the latest operation to restore sight,
loves the scent and sounds of Christmas,
the brilliant red and green letters
she read like tiny pictures just a few days ago,
before they slipped away completely,
and she learned they would not come back.

We reach home, and Dan parks;
As we get out, a taper in the window flickers
its small light for all the changing days,
and the neighbor walking his spaniel
nods a greeting before going in.

## Flesh and Sanity

At lunch, the juice
of a ripe pear trickles
down the white inside of my
arm. You lean over, lick it off.

I flush to remember last night:
your belly and chest against mine,
drawing a chorus of surrenders
to and from my body's contest.

And, just hours from now
you will tell me how you sat
with my scent still on you
at a conference table

with the associate director
and deputy comptroller, pretending
to consider budget options, but
saying to yourself: *I was a mile deep*

*in my woman at lunch,*
and calling us back to this chair,
where I now slip over you like a nesting bird,
pulling and savoring its last pure morsel

of pleasure in that safe place we create
with our bodies, away from the work world's
clicking assertions, back to this moment
of flesh and sanity, sticky with hope.

# Notes

Page 36: According to Frazer's *The New Golden Bough*, Contagious Magic operates by the Law of Contagion or Contact, i.e, things once in contact continue always to act upon each other. A knife that wounds someone must be cleaned and tended for the wound to heal—that sort of thing. Perhaps the wound that rationality can inflict on a fuller way of thinking could double back to enlighten the instruments of reason. As Heidegger said in a different context, "what withdraws in such a manner keeps and develops its own, incomparable nearness."

Page 40: *Atropos, Clotho,* and *Lachesis*—The Three Fates: *Clotho* weaves the thread of life, *Lachesis* measures it out, and *Atropos* clips it at the end with her scissors.

Page 54: The Revere camera provides two images which are mounted side-by-side as slides for use in a viewer. Pushing the button on top lights the viewer, making it possible to see a 3-D image.

Patricia Gray was born in Washington, D.C. and grew up in the Shenandoah Valley, not far from Charlottesville, Virginia. In 1983 she received the M.F.A. degree in poetry from the University of Virginia and was awarded the Academy of American Poets Prize. Since 1994, she has coordinated the Poetry at Noon program at the Library of Congress. She has also taught poetry writing in the Washington area, including a class in modern poetry at the Smithsonian. Her poems have appeared in numerous magazines, such as *Poetry International*, *Poetry East*, *The MacGuffin*, *Shenandoah*, and in the online publications: www.forpoetry.com and www.poetrymagazine.com. In 2000 and 2002, she received artist fellowships in poetry from the D.C. Commission on the Arts and Humanities. She lives and works on Capitol Hill and bothers her son constantly with computer questions.